Winning Business Investments in the United States

1

Winning Business Investment in the United States

PRESIDENT BARACK OBAMA SPEAKING TO 1,300 REPRESENTATIVES OF LOCAL ECONOMIC DEVELOPMENT ORGANIZATIONS AND GLOBAL COMPANIES INTERESTED IN INVESTING IN THE UNITED STATES AT THE SELECTUSA INVESTMENT SUMMIT IN OCTOBER 2013. (OFFICIAL WHITE HOUSE PHOTO BY PETE SOUZA)

The United States is an increasingly attractive location for business investment from global companies. In AT Kearney's 2013 FDI Confidence Index, the United States surged past countries like China, Brazil and India to become the country with the top FDI prospects globally, as ranked by 302 companies representing 28 countries and multiple industry sectors.[1] This marks the first time that the US occupied the #1 spot in the survey since 2001.[2] In a survey of U.S. manufacturers with production abroad late last year, BCG found that the majority (54 percent) are looking at re-shoring to the United States, up from 37 percent in 2012. [3]

More and more companies are choosing to locate here after weighing the United States' competitive advantages, including our:

- *Skills and productivity*: The U.S. workforce is among the most skilled and productive globally – more than 30 percent more productive than Germany's and nearly twice as productive as South Korea's.[4]

- *Innovation:* The United States is the global leader in patents, producing nearly 30 percent of all patents worldwide, and has 15 of the top 25 leading research universities.[5] Not surprisingly, the United States also has over a third of the world's total R&D investment, more than any other country.[6]

- *Energy:* With a century of reserves, natural gas costs one third as much here as it does in Asia and our low energy costs overall are estimated to save U.S. manufacturers nearly $130 billion annually compared to Europe.[7]

- *Access to markets:* Locating in the United States provides unparalleled access to the largest consumer market in the world and rapid access to global markets, with the United States having free trade agreements with 20 other countries and the most rapid export clearances of the 185 countries surveyed by the World Bank.[8]

As the United States becomes increasingly competitive for investment, more global companies, including companies that are foreign-owned, are investing in and creating jobs in America. Business fixed investment from companies choosing to grow and invest in the United States accounts for more than 20 percent of the rebound in real GDP since mid-2009.[9]

While the precise amount of re-shoring from U.S. companies is difficult to track, all signs are that it is growing. And more measureable data on investments and jobs created by foreign companies in the United States provides a powerful proxy for the overall trend of re-shoring and growing U.S. competitiveness for business investment.

Since 2006, the United States has been the world's largest recipient of foreign direct investment (FDI).[10] In 2013, net FDI in the United States, as measured by U.S. assets of foreign affiliates, reached an all-time high totaling $4.6 trillion.[11] And FDI inflows have swelled, totaling $1.5 trillion between 2006 and 2012. For 2013 alone, FDI inflows totaled $193 billion up from $166 billion in 2012.[12] In addition, since 2010, the United States has experienced a step change in its share of total FDI inflows to developed countries, as measured by inflows to the G7, receiving nearly 50 percent of total FDI inflows to these countries annually, a two-thirds larger share than its typical share in prior years.[13]

This investment strengthens our economy: it directly supports well-paying jobs for millions of U.S. workers, paves the way for future business expansion and hiring, expands our exports, transfers innovations and knowledge from around the globe, and funds an outsized share of the nation's research and development. In 2011, global investment, as measured for majority-owned U.S. affiliates of foreign companies[1], represented only 4.7 percent of total U.S. private output, but contributed 15.9 percent of U.S. private research and development spending; more than triple its respective share.[14]

Global investment creates high-paying U.S. jobs. Because global investment is concentrated in the knowledge-intensive, high-skill industries where the United States leads globally, compensation at U.S. affiliates of foreign companies is 33 percent higher than the U.S. average, and is consistently higher than the national average for both manufacturing and non-manufacturing jobs alike.[15]

Global investment accounts for a significant share of jobs and job growth in competitive U.S. industries – like manufacturing, where global investment contributes 18 percent of employment and created 120,000 manufacturing jobs between 2009 and 2011.[16] And this trend is accelerating as the United States becomes more competitive - one third of all manufacturing jobs created in 2011, the most recent year for which we have data, were created by foreign companies choosing to locate production in the United States.[17]

In 2011, the Administration launched SelectUSA, the first-ever U.S. government-wide program to bring jobs and investment from around the world to the United States:

- SelectUSA, operated by the Department of Commerce, makes investment attraction a core priority of the Administration, serving as a single point of contact for ready investors, coordinating investment advocacy all the way up to the President and providing services and support for U.S. regions and communities to compete globally for investment.

- In just over two years, SelectUSA facilitated over $18 billion in new investment for the United States

---

[1] Data on the U.S. output, assets, and employment of majority-owned U.S. affiliates of foreign companies, used throughout this report is also referred to here as global investment.

- SelectUSA will provide services to nearly 1,000 potential investors and economic development organizations this year alone, advising them on the advantages of investing in the United States and helping them navigate the process.

Looking ahead, we need to continue to nurture and build upon the underlying strengths of the U.S. economy, and harness programs such as SelectUSA so that even more companies will choose to invest and grow in the United States.

SECTION 1:
THE U.S. IS INCREASINGLY COMPETITIVE FOR GLOBAL INVESTMENT

The United States' Competitive Advantages

The United States is highly competitive globally as a destination for investment. In AT Kearney's 2013 FDI Confidence Index, the United States surged past countries like China, Brazil and India to become the country with the top FDI prospects globally, as ranked by 302 companies representing 28 countries and multiple industry sectors.[18] This marks the first time that the United States occupied the #1 spot in the survey since 2001.[19]

A number of growing advantages make the United States a winning destination for investment including:

- One of the most highly skilled and productive workforces in the world
- Global leadership in innovation and invention
- A booming energy sector and low-cost natural gas and electricity
- Rapid access to domestic and global markets

Businesses are waking up to value of the United States' competitive advantages, even over low-wage locations. In the past, low wages and cost competitiveness were considered synonymous, with businesses "chasing low wages" in making decisions about where to invest, regardless of skill and productivity differences between the low-wage and American workforces. However, experience in low-wage countries has imparted a more nuanced view. Businesses have learned that today's low wages may be gone tomorrow and that other costs and risks often offset the savings from cheap labor. As a result, more businesses are taking a fresh look at the advantages the United States holds for investment.

A Skilled and Highly Productive Workforce

The U.S. workforce is among the most highly skilled and innovative in the world. The United Nations Development Program ranks the United States first in the world in average years of schooling, a global measure for richness of human capital.[20] The United States' strong education and training system including high schools, community colleges and four-year institutions provides a national infrastructure for job-driven training and has been strengthened by Administration efforts, including a fresh infusion of more than $2 billion, to ensure the availability of skilled workers for all firms operating in the United States.[21] Not surprisingly given its high degree of skills, the U.S. workforce is among the most productive in the world – more than 30 percent more productive than Germany's and nearly twice as productive as South Korea's workforce.[22] And the U.S. workforce is set to maintain this significant advantage thanks to ongoing productivity growth.

Global Leadership in Innovation

The United States is the world's leading source of innovation and invention. Fifteen of the top 25 research universities in the world and many more top-flight research institutions are located in the United States.[23] These universities and institutions are essential partners for companies making R&D investments here like GLOBALFOUNDRIES, which located a $2 billion Technology Development Center in upstate New York in part to access nearby research partnerships. The United States ranks among the top five on the World Intellectual Property Organization's rankings in both investment in knowledge as a share of GDP and in innovation. 33.8 percent of world R&D investments are made in the United States.[24] Moreover, the United States retains its lead as the world's most inventive country in 2013, accounting for 27.9 percent of all international patent applications among 148 nations.[25]

And companies locating in the United States for access to innovation can rest assured that their investments in research and their discoveries will be protected through our strong and accessible system for intellectual property protection. Government fees for obtaining a U.S. patent are among the lowest in the industrialized world and discounted fees are available for small and medium sized entities.[26] While there is still more that we need to do to ensure that our patent system creates the right incentives to encourage innovation and invention, this intellectual property regime is just one example of the stable and predictable regulatory environment that the United States has to offer. A predictable regulatory environment, in turn, makes doing business easier. In 2013, the World Bank ranked the United States fourth out of 185 countries in terms of the "ease of doing business".[27]

Booming Energy Sector

Increased domestic energy production has brought down prices and brightened the U.S. energy outlook, most notably for natural gas. Between 2007 and 2012, U.S. prices for natural gas dropped nearly 60 percent as production rose and new reserves were uncovered. In contrast, the northern European or Asian spot markets post prices ranging from twice to several times the prices paid in the United States.[28] The country's natural gas boom has catalyzed domestic and foreign investment in petrochemical manufacturing as well as in the manufacturing of steel and equipment needed for gas extraction. Indeed petrochemical companies have announced over $80 billion of planned investments in the United States, taking advantage of this low-cost energy and feedstocks.[29] Multiple industries benefit directly from inexpensive U.S.-produced natural gas because of its diverse industrial uses, ranging from on-site electricity generation to process heating, space heating, steam generation, and petrochemical processing. The International Energy Agency estimates that in 2012 alone, lower gas and electricity prices in the United States versus Europe saved the U.S. manufacturing industry close to $130 billion.[30]

In addition, rapidly growing domestic demand for renewable energy offers opportunities for firms to produce in the United States to serve this demand and to offset high shipping costs for heavy parts such as wind turbine towers and blades. Since 2008, the amount of solar power installed in the U.S. has increased nearly 11-fold, to an estimated 13 gigawatts.[31] 72 percent of wind turbine components installed in the United States in 2012, such as towers, blades, and gears, were made in America, nearly tripling the 25 percent domestic share in 2006-2007.[32]

Figure 1: Natural Gas Prices in the United States, United Kingdom, and Japan
($ per million Btu)

Source: McKinsey Global Institute. Game Changers: *Game Changers: Five opportunities for U.S. Growth and Renewal.* July 2013.

A recent study finds that access to markets is one of the factors driving the decisions of multinationals to locate in the United States.[33] The U.S. economy is the largest in the world, and with a median household income of $51,371 in 2012[34], offers a large and steady demand for a variety of products. A policy of "build where you sell" allows firms to gain deep insight into how local consumers use a firm's product, uses that may differ significantly from those in a multinational's home market. And locating in the United States to serve U.S. demand allows companies to react quickly to increased data on demand to get ahead of the competition, while also avoiding dozens of hidden costs. Examples of such costs include the long trips and time of top executives required to communicate with suppliers abroad, risk associated with uncertainty in shipping prices and delivery times and difficulty in verifying product quality over long supply chains.

While we have more to do to keep pace with other countries when it comes to investing in our infrastructure, the United States possesses a legacy of world-class ports plus freight rail, air transportation, and road networks capable of not only serving the large U.S. market but making the United States a base for exports as well. U.S. regulations for exporting are also among the easiest in the world. Specifically, the United States requires the least amount of time to comply with all procedures for exporting goods among 185 countries surveyed by the World Bank.[35] The United States also has free trade agreements in place with 20 countries and a host of bilateral investment treaties that promote exports.[36] And the Administration is working to open up additional markets to U.S. exports through trade agreements that are on the way. U.S. affiliates of foreign firms take advantage of this access to global markets - accounting for a significant share of total U.S. exports. For example, in 2011, U.S. affiliates of foreign firms exported $303.7 billion of goods, accounting for 20.5 percent of total U.S. goods exports, the second highest share since 1995.[37]

Figure 2: Exports of Goods by Majority-owned U.S. Affiliates of Foreign Firms, 1997-2011

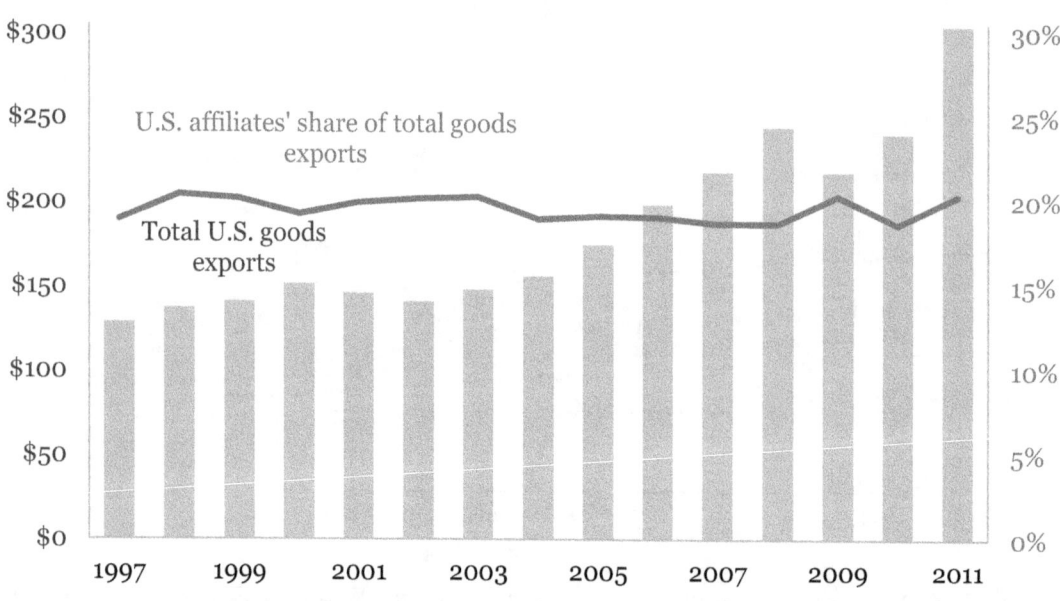

Source: Department of Commerce, Bureau of Economic Analysis
Note: Data prior to 2007 do not include U.S. affiliates of foreign banks.

Businesses are Increasing Investment in the United States

Recent studies have demonstrated that global businesses see the United States as an increasingly competitive place in which to invest. The Organization for International Investment (OFII) and PricewaterhouseCoopers LLP (PwC) recently presented findings from their 2014 Insourcing Survey, showing significant confidence in the United States as a location for companies and supply chains.[38] The survey showed that 51 percent of global companies with U.S. operations plan to increase U.S. employment in 2014 and 64 percent plan to increase their investment in the United States this year.

The Boston Consulting Group (BCG) in a 2013 survey similarly found that more than half (54 percent) of executives at U.S.-based manufacturing companies with sales greater than $1 billion are considering re-shoring production to the United States – up from 37 percent in 2012.[39] BCG further found a doubling since 2012 in the share of U.S.-based executives who are actively shifting production from China to the United States.

The attractiveness of the United States for investment is also evidenced by the fact that the United States consistently ranks as one of the top destinations in the world for investment and has been the largest recipient of foreign direct investment since 2006, with investment inflows totaling more than $1.5 trillion through 2012. And more recently, the United States has experienced a step change in its share of foreign direct investment inflows to developed countries – with half of all inflows to G7 countries destined for the United States.[40]

These investments further strengthen the U.S. economy: they support well-paying jobs for millions of U.S. workers, expand our exports, and fund research and development.

Foreign Direct Investment in the United States is Substantial

Precise data on the amount of investment U.S. firms have returned to the U.S. from abroad, or kept in the U.S., are difficult to assess, but investment by foreign firms into the United States, an easier-to-quantify proxy for the United States overall competitiveness is substantial and growing.

- In 2013, net U.S. assets of foreign affiliates totaled $4.6 trillion and FDI inflows totaled $193 billion.[41]

- In 2012, the U.S. manufacturing sector accounted for approximately 50 percent of the total share of FDI dollars flowing into the United States, led by pharmaceuticals and petroleum and coal products. Outside manufacturing, wholesale trade accounted for 12 percent, while mining, non-bank holding companies, finance and insurance, and banking accounted for the bulk of the remaining 38 percent of total foreign investment.[42]

- Since 2010, Japan, Canada, Australia, Korea, and seven European countries collectively have accounted for more than 80 percent of new FDI into the United States.[43] Although still small, investment flows from emerging economies are growing rapidly.

- Since 2010, the United States has experienced a step change in its share of FDI inflows to developed countries, as measured by inflows to the G7, receiving a nearly 50 percent share of total FDI inflows to developed countries annually. More than two-thirds higher than its typical share of developed country FDI inflows in prior years.[44]

Figure 3: U.S. Share of FDI Inflows to G7 Countries: 2002-2013
(Percent of total inflows to G7 countries, trailing three year average)

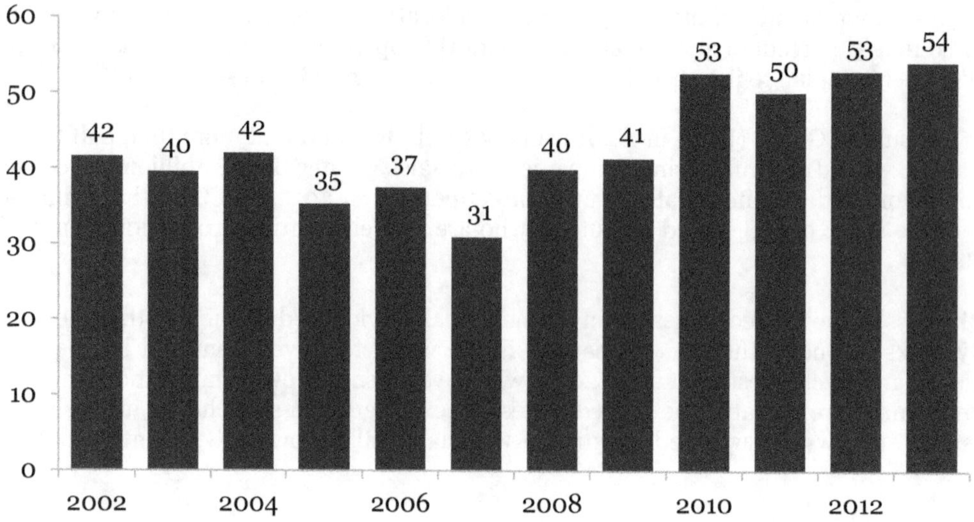

Source: OECD. Investment Statistics. April 2014. Note: G7 countries include Canada, France, Germany, Italy, Japan, the United Kingdom, and the United States.

Global Investment Benefits the U.S. Economy

"Because we bet on this country, suddenly foreign companies are, too. Right now, more of Honda's cars are made in America than anyplace else on Earth. Airbus, the European aircraft company, they're building new planes in Alabama. And American companies like Ford are replacing outsourcing with insourcing -- they're bringing jobs back home."

- *President Barack Obama, Knox College July, 2013*

As the President explained, fostering strong demand and a productive business environment in turn attracts investment, together contributing to strong economic performance. Business investment is a key source of capital, employment, innovation, and cross-border trade. In the United States, business investments have led to the creation of competitive jobs, investments in fixed assets and research and development, and overall growth and innovation that drives U.S. competitiveness.

Since President Obama's Knox College speech, the number of private sector jobs has increased by nearly 1.8 million, making the total number of jobs over the past 50 months 9.2 million private sector jobs —with 647,000 in our nation's factories. Business investment has also been robust. In 2013, business fixed investment, measured as nonresidential fixed investment, totaled over $2 trillion and accounted for more than 20 percent of the rebound in real GDP since mid-2009.[45]

Foreign direct investment is a prominent feature of the U.S. economic landscape and further highlights the role of business investment in economic performance. Inbound direct investment funds a number of types of physical assets, including production plants, research and development (R&D) facilities, sales offices, warehouses, and service centers. It can take the form of a "greenfield" establishment that creates new operations or a merger or acquisition ("M&A") of a sufficiently large stake in an existing enterprise. Whatever the form, it ultimately translates into output, jobs, exports, R&D, and growth of the U.S. economy.

9

Global investment, as represented by majority-owned U.S. affiliates of foreign companies, creates high-paying U.S. jobs – because their employment is concentrated in high-skill occupations, compensation at U.S. affiliates of foreign companies has been consistently higher than the U.S. average and is true for both manufacturing and non-manufacturing jobs.

U.S. affiliates of foreign firms employed 5.6 million people in the United States, or 5.1 percent of private sector employment, in 2011.[46] Consistent with estimates of the investment position by industry, about one-third of jobs at U.S. affiliates are in the manufacturing sector.

In 2011, manufacturing employment at U.S. affiliates of international firms was 2.1 million, or 17.8 percent of all U.S. manufacturing employment. Foreign companies investing in the United States created 120,000 manufacturing jobs between 2009 and 2011.[47] And this trend has accelerated - one third of all manufacturing jobs created in 2011, the latest year for which we have data, were from foreign companies choosing to locate production here.[48]

 Next to manufacturing, the largest industry sectors for employment by U.S. affiliates are wholesale trade which employed 546,600 workers, representing 9.9percent of total employment within the wholesale trade sector, retail trade with 488,500, representing 3.3percent of total employment within the retail trade sector; and administration, support, and waste management with 482,200 workers, representing 6.2percent of total employment within this sector.[49]

Because global investment is concentrated in the knowledge-intensive, high-skilled industries in which the United States has a global edge, U.S. affiliates tend to hire highly skilled workers and pay excellent wages. These firms paid wages and other forms of compensation that averaged more than $77,000 per U.S. employee in 2011 as compared to average earnings of $58,000 for workers in the economy as a whole.[50] Compensation at U.S. affiliates has been consistently higher than the U.S. average over time, and the differential holds for both manufacturing and non-manufacturing jobs, with a slightly higher differential in manufacturing.

Figure 4: Annual Compensation per Employee, 2011

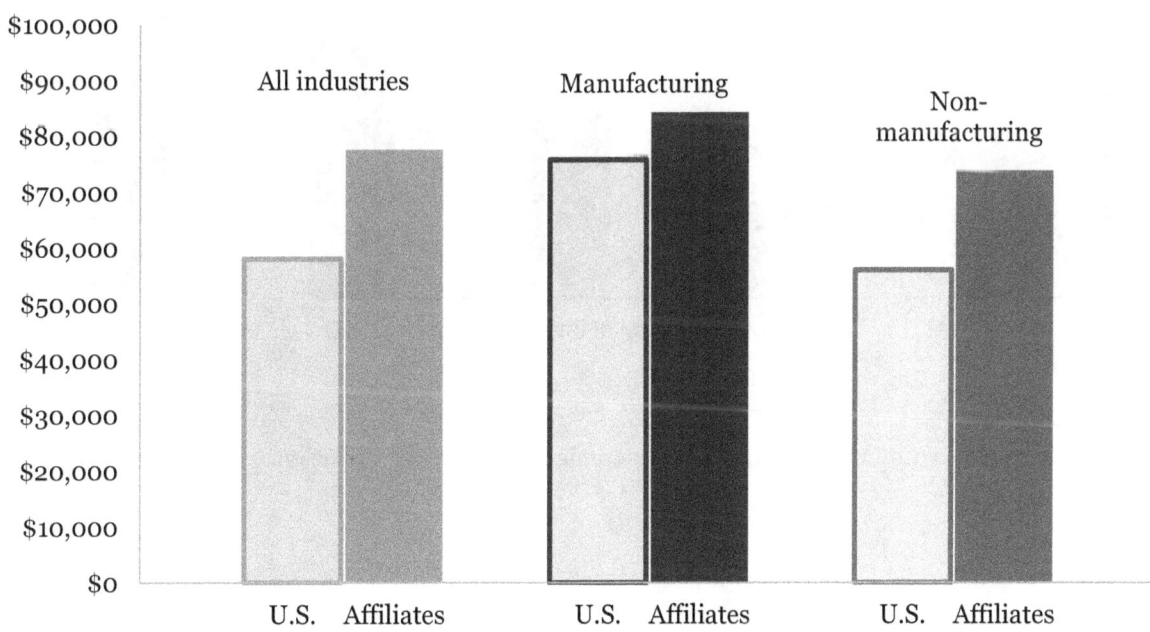

Global Investment Punches above its Weight in Output And R&D

In 2011, global investment, as measured by the activities of U.S. affiliates of foreign firms, accounted for only 4.7 percent of total U.S. private output, but contributed 9.6 percent of U.S. private investment and 15.9 percent of U.S. private research and development spending; more than nearly double and triple its respective share. U.S. affiliates are also well-integrated globally and are the source of 20.5 percent of total U.S. goods exports.[51]

Global investment's share of U.S. research and investment is rising. In 2011, these firms spent $45.2 billion on R&D, accounting for 15.9 percent of total R&D spending by businesses.[52] Since 1997, when the data were first published, R&D expenditures of U.S. affiliates have climbed 163 percent, close to double the 87 percent growth among overall business spending on R&D. The bulk of the R&D investments were in the manufacturing sector, which accounted for 69.9 percent of total R&D expenditures by U.S. affiliates. Affiliates in the wholesale trade sector spent $7.0 billion on R&D in 2011, followed by the professional, scientific, and technical services sector ($4.1 billion), and the information sector ($1.5 billion).

Figure 5: Economic Activity of Majority-Owned U.S. Affiliates of Foreign Companies, 2011

(Percent total for the U.S. economy)

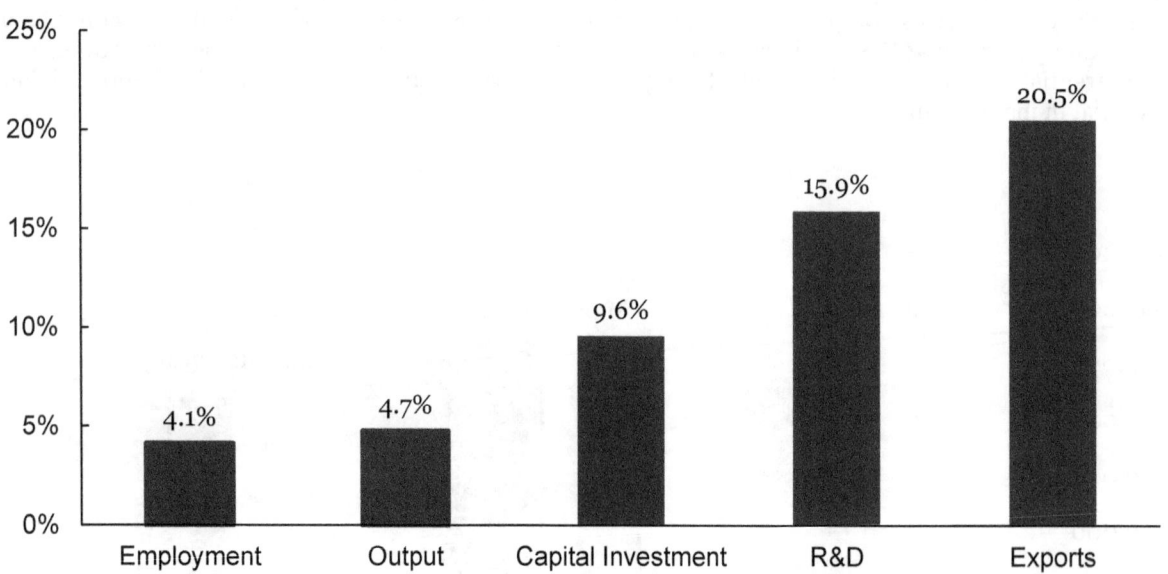

Source: Department of Commerce, Bureau of Economic Analysis; National Science Foundation

SECTION 2
SelectUSA SUCCESS AND SERVICES

SelectUSA: The First-Ever Government-Wide Program to Compete for Jobs and Investment in the United States

President Obama established SelectUSA in 2011 by Executive Order as the first-ever U.S. government-wide program to promote and facilitate business investment in the United States. SelectUSA competes to bring jobs and investment from around the world to the United States by making investment attraction a core priority of the Administration, actively encouraging companies around the world to consider the United States, serving as a single point of contact for ready investors, coordinating investment advocacy all the way up to the President and providing services and support for U.S. regions and communities to compete globally for investment.

The SelectUSA team is housed within the Department of Commerce, and coordinates with more than 20 federal agencies to respond to potential investors and help them navigate the U.S. federal system. SelectUSA provides advice and services to foreign investors of all sizes, domestic companies considering reshoring, and U.S. state, regional and local economic development organizations (EDOs).

On October 31, 2013, President Obama and Secretary Penny Pritzker opened the SelectUSA 2013 Investment Summit. They were joined by Secretary of State John Kerry, Secretary of the Treasury Jacob Lew, Secretary of Labor Thomas Perez, and U.S. Trade Representative Michael Froman to warmly welcome a full house of 1,300 attendees. Forty-eight states, four territories and the District of Columbia participated to share investment opportunities with more than 650 international participants from 60 different markets.

At the Summit, President Obama announced a series of commitments to enhance and expand SelectUSA's efforts. The commitments – and SelectUSA's progress – are reported below.

- *Making investment attraction a core priority of the Administration, with coordinated, global teams actively working to facilitate investment.* The Department of Commerce and the Department of State have been working together to fulfill this commitment, providing the training, resources, and access necessary to fully incorporate investment promotion and facilitation as a core element of U.S. economic and commercial efforts. For example, in the 32 foreign markets that account for the lion's share of FDI into the United States, coordinated teams have developed and are implementing localized action plans to target likely investors and persuade them to locate in the United States.

- *Strengthening SelectUSA's role as a single point of contact for ready investors looking to create jobs and establish production in the United States.* As part of this effort, SelectUSA has designed and implemented a formalized ombudsman service in partnership with more than 20 federal government agencies. The ombudsman service assists international investors, U.S. investors considering re-shoring, and EDOs to navigate the federal regulatory system and includes clear channels for referrals and case-management processes. Training has been provided for agency representatives, and the process has already been put into action. SelectUSA assists investors and EDOs with questions related to the federal rules and regulations that govern investments and federal economic development resources. Investments are time sensitive, so SelectUSA can identify the right office within the federal government to ensure that investors receive answers in a timely manner.

- *Coordinating an investment advocacy process all the way up to the President.* SelectUSA has created a formal process for engaging all levels of government, including senior government officials to advocate for business investment in the United States when U.S. jurisdictions are competing against foreign locations. For example, the President on overseas trips now meets with potential investors through SelectUSA to advocate for the United States. And when competing for investment, SelectUSA can call on the energies of the most senior officials just as it called on Vice President Biden and Commerce Secretary Pritzker to advocate for an investment from Lufthansa in Puerto Rico. As U.S. state, regional and local economic development organizations compete against foreign jurisdictions for jobs, the U.S. federal government stands ready to assist. During advocacy cases, investors often raise questions that can be addressed through SelectUSA's ombudsman process, so increased advocacy ultimately also improves SelectUSA's responsiveness to investors.

- *Providing increased and more coordinated support for states and localities to attract investment.* SelectUSA continues to assist state, regional, and local EDOs to attract investment, and is improving this service through better interagency and international cooperation. This includes higher profile, international events to facilitate direct connections between EDOs and investors (see box below). Furthermore, SelectUSA is significantly increasing its efforts to engage national associations and other partners to reach more economic developers at the local, regional and state levels. EDOs will have more opportunities to share their stories with investors. Investors will have more (and more convenient) opportunities to meet representatives of EDOs.

SelectUSA Global Events and Road Shows Promoting the United States

SelectUSA has hit the road internationally to spread the good news about the United States as a competitive place for investment. In the first five months of 2014, SelectUSA has held more fifteen events targeting global investors to raise their interest in investing in the United States.

SelectUSA's investment events in 2014:

January 2014
- SelectUSA Seminars (Sendai and Fukuoka, Japan)

March 2014
- Japan SelectUSA Launch and Showcase (Tokyo, Japan)
- Korea SelectUSA Roundtable and Delegation (Seoul, South Korea)
- SelectUSA for Startups in London (London, United Kingdom)
- USA: A Market in Strong Recovery (Naples and Bari, Italy)
-

April 2014
- Austrian Investment Forums (Vienna and Linz, Austria)
- USA Investment Center Pavilion (Hannover, Germany)
- Pearl River Delta SelectUSA Road Show (Hong Kong, Shenzhen, and Guangzhou, China)
- Invest in America Seminar (Belgium, Netherlands, France)
- SelectUSA CEO Roundtables (Tokyo, Japan, Seoul, South Korea)

May 2014
- Turkish American Business Council Seminar (Istanbul, Turkey)
- "Formulating Your company's Aeronautics / Electronics Investment" (Toulouse, France)
- SelectUSA Workshop for Small and Medium-Sized Companies (Düsseldorf, Germany)
- Korea SelectUSA Road Show (Seoul, South Korea)
- Japan SelectUSA Road Show (Tokyo, Nagoya and Osaka, Japan)

Coming Soon in 2014
- More events in Mexico, Israel, Switzerland, China, Canada, Germany, Chile, Brazil, Colombia, Australia, and New Zealand.

Details on upcoming activities can be found at www.SelectUSA.gov or by contacting the SelectUSA office.

Services for Investors and U.S. Economic Development Organizations

SelectUSA serves as an information clearinghouse for the global investment community, an ombudsman for investors, and an advocate for U.S. cities, states, and regions. SelectUSA's services for investors and economic development organizations (EDOs) include:

o   *Information Assistance for Investors:* SelectUSA provides information to international investors and U.S. companies considering re-shoring on the benefits of establishing operations in the United States, as well as the information needed to move investments forward. Investors need to understand how the U.S. system and regulations work and they need facts, data and local contacts which SelectUSA can provide.

o   *Counseling and Information for U.S. EDOs:* SelectUSA works closely with U.S. EDOs at the state, regional and local levels to provide counseling on strategy and best practices to attract foreign direct investment and companies considering re-shoring. SelectUSA can leverage resources from U.S. embassies and consulates across more than 120 international markets to provide information and advice.

o   *Global Platform for Promotion:* SelectUSA provides on-the-ground assistance for EDOs with Single Location Promotion events in foreign markets. SelectUSA leads regular investment Road Shows and seminars in key markets, as well as U.S. pavilions at high-profile international trade shows, to bring EDOs and investors face to face.

o   *Ombudsman Services:* SelectUSA coordinates federal agencies through the Interagency Investment Working Group to address investor questions and concerns relating to a wide range of federal regulatory issues. SelectUSA aims to ensure investors understand the U.S. system and receive answers in the timely manner.

o   *Investment Advocacy:* U.S. state and local governments often find themselves competing with a foreign location for a project. SelectUSA wants to do its best to bring those potential jobs to the United States, so SelectUSA coordinates senior U.S. government officials to advocate on behalf of the United States for investment.

To request SelectUSA services, please visit www.SelectUSA.gov or contact your nearest U.S. Embassy or consulate.

Recent SelectUSA Successes

In just over two years, SelectUSA has facilitated over $18 billion in new investment for the United States. And SelectUSA is set to win even more investment for the United States in the months ahead. In this fiscal year, SelectUSA will provide services to nearly 1,000 investors and EDOs to advocate for business investments in the United States.

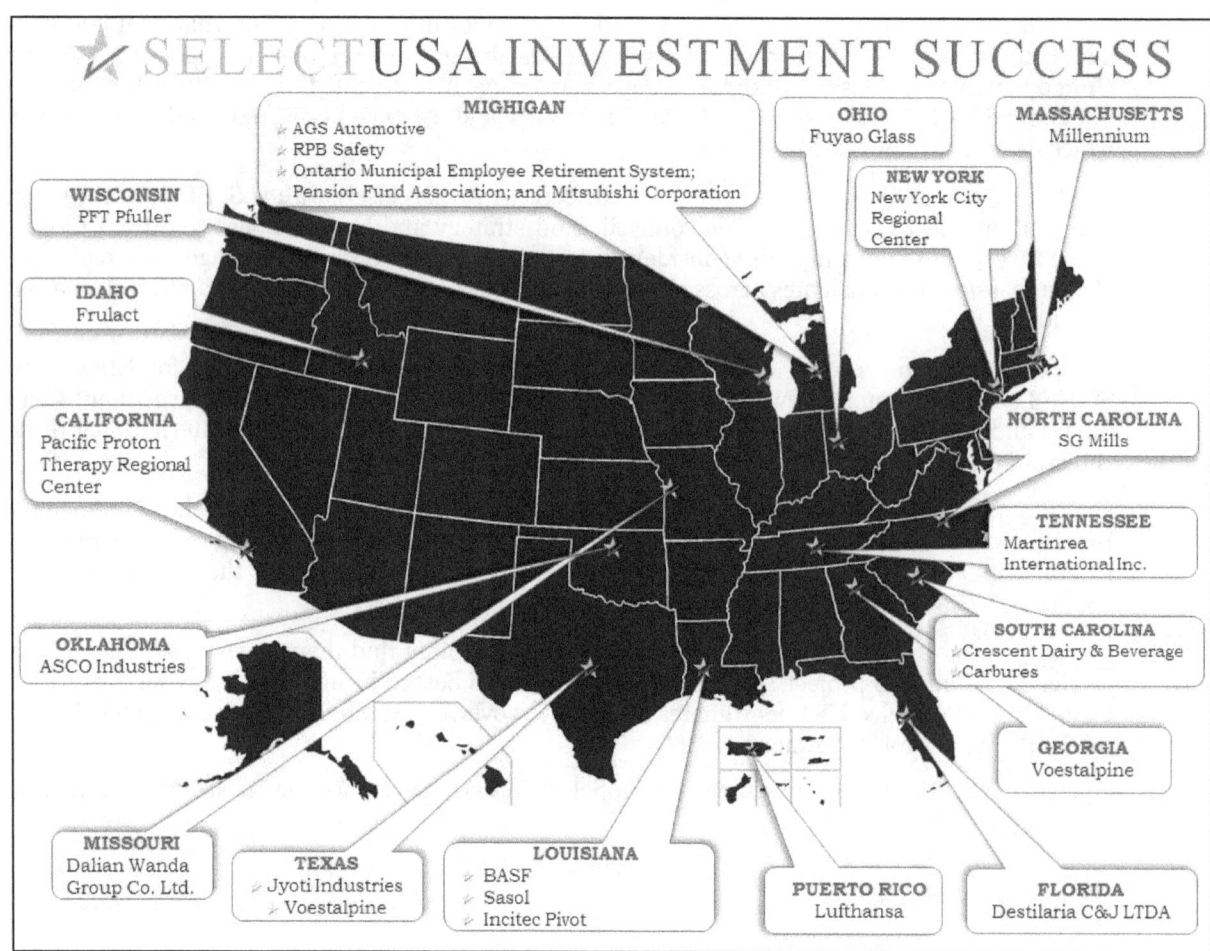

SelectUSA has played a substantial role in investment wins across the country, such as investments in Rupert, Idaho, by the FRULACT Group, and in Moraine, Ohio by the Fuyao Glass Industry Group. As detailed below, spring 2014 has brought notable new investments by Lufthansa Technik in Puerto Rico, by SG Mills in North Carolina and by The Richelieu Group in the Southeast.

The Richelieu Group

Richelieu is a legwear company—maker of brands such as Peds, Coolfeet, and Growing Socks—originally founded in Sorel, Québec in 1934. In 2011, Richelieu invested $ 7 million in Burke County, North Carolina to rescue a failing sock company named International Legwear Group (ILG). Within 10 days of ILG announcing its liquidation, Richelieu stepped in, re-hiring 45 workers that had been laid off and saving the company's ongoing accounts. Today, in an area hard-hit by the recession, the business is thriving and the workforce has nearly doubled.

Richelieu is now increasing its investment and will soon announce the U.S. location of a new state-of-the-art facility that will re-shore production and ultimately create more than 200 new jobs. The investment will be approximately $9 million initially, with an additional $15 million planned for a second phase. The new facility will manufacture socks to be sold across the country, as well as in Canada, Mexico and Korea. Richelieu has worked closely with Walmart, one of its major customers, which has played a pivotal role encouraging the company's efforts by signing a multi-year commitment and providing support throughout the planning process.

SelectUSA, through the U.S. Commercial Service in Canada, has also been instrumental by assisting the company navigate the intricacies of federal regulations for investing in the United States. CS Canada began engaging with Richelieu in 2012 by providing comprehensive counselling on the U.S. economic, business, and investment climate. Additional support was provided to the company on federal regulations such as immigration and work permits, and on potential sources of capital.

"Our experience operating in the United States has been an unqualified success. We're thriving and expanding thanks to the quality of our employees and the ease of doing business. The service and support we've received from SelectUSA through the teams in both Canada and the United States has also made a real difference. " Mr. Michael D. Penner, President and CEO, Richelieu

Lufthansa Technik

In April 2014, Lufthansa Technik, a provider of maintenance, repair, and overhaul services for aircraft, engines, and component parts, announced a significant investment in the Commonwealth of Puerto Rico. Lufthansa Technik is a subsidiary of the Lufthansa Group, which comprises several businesses and accounts for 10,000 employees in the United States.

Lufthansa Technik chose the United States—among strong international competition—as the site of a new aviation maintenance, repair and overhaul facility to service short-haul and medium-haul aircraft. The company expects to create up to 400 permanent jobs. Local efforts to recruit the investment were led by Governor Alejandro García Padilla and the Puerto Rico Industrial Development Company.

With the support of Vice President Biden, the White House National Economic Council, and the President's Task Force on Puerto Rico, the SelectUSA team at the U.S. Department of Commerce worked with Puerto Rico to offer Lufthansa information and assistance from across federal agencies and departments. SelectUSA's efforts not only assisted Lufthansa Technik in making its decision, but also demonstrated why the United States is the top destination for foreign direct investment.

"We are very proud to establish with our partner a new overhaul facility in Puerto Rico and grow our presence in the United States. This Lufthansa Group investment was brought forth with intense due diligence and cooperation to ensure our long-term success and mutual commitment to excellence, and we look forward to continuing this important partnership." Mr. August Henningsen, CEO, Lufthansa Technik

SG Mills

Shri Govindaraja Textiles Private Limited (SG Mills), part of the Jayavilas Group in Aruppukottai, India, is a third-generation, family-owned business. The group's core business is textiles, but it also has interests in several other industries. SG Mills is the largest spinner in India with a total installed capacity of 1.1 million spindles and a workforce of 30,000 employees.

On May 1, 2014, Governor Pat McCrory announced that SG Mills will open its first U.S.-based operation in Eden, North Carolina. The company plans to invest more than $40 million and create 84 jobs during the next two years.

SelectUSA, through the U.S. Commercial Service post in Chennai, India, worked closely with the team members at SG Mills as they considered their approach to the U.S. market.

"I sincerely thank the support offered by the State Commerce Department, Eden City officials, US Commercial Service officials, and the Consul General at the American Consulate in Chennai, India for really helping us expedite the search, selection, and commencement process." Mr. Ramkumar Varadarajan, Managing Director, SG Mills

Notes

Section 1 draws extensively from http://www.whitehouse.gov/sites/default/files/docs/cea-doc 2013 foreign direct investment in the us.pdf. Unless otherwise noted, statistics are drawn from this report.

SelectUSA exercises strict geographic neutrality, and represents the entire United States. The program does not promote one U.S. location over another U.S. location.

[1] AT Kearney, Foreign Direct Investment Confidence Index, 2013. http://www.atkearney.com/documents/10192/1464437/Back+to+Business+-+Optimism+Amid+Uncertainty+-+FDICI+2013.pdf/96039e18-5d34-49ca-9cec-5c1f27dc099d

[2] Ibid.

[3] Boston Consulting Group. Majority of Large Manufacturers Are Now Planning or Considering 'Reshoring' from China to the U.S. http://www.bcg.com/media/pressreleasedetails.aspx?id=tcm:12-144944.

[4] The Conference Board Total Economy Database™, January 2014, http://www.conference-board.org/data/economydatabase/

[5] World Intellectual Property Organization. Press Release March 2014. http://www.wipo.int/pressroom/en/articles/2014/article_0002.html.; Times Higher Education World Reputation Rankings 2014. http://www.theguardian.com/news/datablog/2014/mar/06/worlds-top-100-universities-2014-reputations-ranked-times-higher-education.

[6] Batelle. Global R&D Funding Forecast 2013. www.battelle.org

[7] McKinsey Global Institute. *Game Changers: Five opportunities for U.S. Growth and Renewal.* July 2013.; World Energy Outlook 2013 Factsheet. http://www.iea.org/media/files/WEO2013_factsheets.pdf.

[8] World Bank. Doing Business Project. *Time to Export.* http://data.worldbank.org/indicator/IC.EXP.DURS

[9] Department of Commerce Bureau of Economic Analysis. National Income and Product Accounts. Also see http://selectusa.commerce.gov/sites/selectusa.commerce.gov/files/documents/2014/january/2013-12-31 selectusa report - fdi in the united states.pdf

[10] Department of Commerce Bureau of Economic Analysis.

[11] United Nations.

[12] Department of Commerce Bureau of Economic Analysis. Direct Investment and MNCs. http://www.bea.gov/international/index.htm#omc. Under an alternative measure, FDI grew from $160.6 billion in 2012 to $187.5 billion in 2013.

[13] OECD. Investment Statistics Long FDI Series. www.oecd.org/investment/statistics. April 2014.

[14] Bureau of Economic Analysis. Direct Investment and MNCs. http://www.bea.gov/international/index.htm#omc

[15] Bureau of Economic Analysis. Direct Investment and MNCs. http://www.bea.gov/international/index.htm#omc

[16] Department of Labor, Bureau of Labor Statistics. Department of Commerce, Bureau of Economic Analysis.

[17] Department of Labor, Bureau of Labor Statistics. Department of Commerce, Bureau of Economic Analysis.

[18] AT Kearney, Foreign Direct Investment Confidence Index, 2013. http://www.atkearney.com/documents/10192/1464437/Back+to+Business+-+Optimism+Amid+Uncertainty+-+FDICI+2013.pdf/96039e18-5d34-49ca-9cec-5c1f27dc099d

[19] Ibid.

[20] United Nations Development Program. See https://data.undp.org/dataset/Mean-years-of-schooling-of-adults-years-/m67k-vi5c for average years of schooling in other countries.

[21] See http://www.whitehouse.gov/blog/2014/05/06/taking-action-attract-world-s-top-talented-professionals for a discussion of Administration policies to attract top talent.

[22] The Conference Board Total Economy Database™, January 2014, http://www.conference-board.org/data/economydatabase/

[23] Times Higher Education World Reputation Rankings 2014. http://www.theguardian.com/news/datablog/2014/mar/06/worlds-top-100-universities-2014-reputations-ranked-times-higher-education.

[24] Batelle. Global R&D Funding Forecast 2013. www.battelle.org

[25] World Intellectual Property Organization. Press Release March 2014. http://www.wipo.int/pressroom/en/articles/2014/article_0002.html

[26] United States Patent and Trademark Office See http://www.uspto.gov/aia_implementation/20120113-ippr_report.pdf.

[27] World Bank Doing Business Project. See http://www.doingbusiness.org/~/media/GIAWB/Doingpercent20Business/Documents/Annual-Reports/English/DB13-full-report.pdf.

[28] Department of Commerce. See http://acetool.commerce.gov/other-inputs.

[29] Industry announcements.

[30] World Energy Outlook 2013 Factsheet. http://www.iea.org/media/files/WEO2013_factsheets.pdf.

[31] Energy Information Administration. http://www.eia.gov/todayinenergy/detail.cfm?id=15751

[32] Department of Energy. See http://energy.gov/articles/energy-dept-reports-us-wind-energy-production-and-manufacturing-reaches-record-highs.

[33] Friedman, J., Gerlowski, D.A., Silberman, J., 2006. "What Attracts Foreign Multinational Corporations? Evidence from Branch Plant Location in the United States," Journal of Regional Science 32(4), 403-418.

[34] Census Bureau. http://www.census.gov/prod/2013pubs/acsbr12-02.pdf.

[35] Department of Commerce. http://acetool.commerce.gov/regulatory-compliance-costs.

[36] United States Trade Representative. http://www.ustr.gov/trade-agreements.

[37] Department of Commerce, Bureau of Economic Analysis.

[38] OFFI and PWC. Insourcing Survey, 2014 http://www.pwc.com/en_US/us/tax-services-multinationals/assets/pwc-insourcing-survey-full-findings-2014.pdf.

[39] Boston Consulting Group. Majority of Large Manufacturers Are Now Planning or Considering 'Reshoring' from China to the U.S. http://www.bcg.com/media/pressreleasedetails.aspx?id=tcm:12-144944.

[40] OECD. Investment Statistics Long FDI Series. www.oecd.org/investment/statistics. April 2014.

[41] Department of Commerce, Bureau of Economic Analysis.

[42] Ibid.

[43] These seven European countries, in descending order of direct investment in the U.S. from 2010 to 2012, are: the United Kingdom, Switzerland, Luxembourg, the Netherlands, Germany, France, and Belgium.

[44] OECD. Investment Statistics Long FDI Series. www.oecd.org/investment/statistics. April 2014.

[45] Department of Commerce Bureau of Economic Analysis. See http://www.bea.gov/iTable/iTable.cfm?ReqID=9&step=1#reqid=9&step=3&isuri=1&903=137 for data on nonresidential fixed investment and http://www.clevelandfed.org/research/trends/2014/0214/ET_feb14.pdf for its contribution to growth in gross domestic product.

[46] Department of Commerce, Bureau of Economic Analysis.

[47] Department of Commerce, Bureau of Economic Analysis and Department of Labor Bureau of Labor Statistics.

[48] Department of Commerce, Bureau of Economic Analysis and Department of Labor Bureau of Labor Statistics.

[49] Department of Commerce, Bureau of Economic Analysis and Department of Labor Bureau of Labor Statistics.

[50] Ibid.

[51] Ibid.

[52] R&D data for affiliates are sourced from the Bureau of Economic Analysis and on all U.S. businesses are sourced from the National Science Foundation.

www.ingramcontent.com/pod-product-compliance
Lightning Source LLC
Chambersburg PA
CBHW080631180526
45168CB00007B/3123